MORNING WAKE UP CALLS

MORNING WAKE UP CALLS

Born Free

ALSO, by **Born Free**

The Book of Born Free
The Wisdom of Living Right Now! Vol. 1

Panther Poetry
(Poems inspired by The Black Panther movie
and the original Black Panther Party)

BUY @ linktr.ee/therealbornfree

God gave you a voice, use it!

Morning Wake Up Calls

Written by Carl **Born Free** Wharton

All rights reserved. This book or any portion thereof may not be reproduced or used in any manner whatsoever without the express written permission of the author/publisher except for the use of brief quotations in a book review or scholarly journal.

Front and back covers created and manifested by
Safiya Wharton of QVision
follow on IG and Fiverr @
https://www.instagram.com/qvision223/
https://www.fiverr.com/qvision223

Graphic design by Wallace Ford
Overseen by **Safiya Wharton**

ISBN: 978-0-578-51074-3

Second edition
Copyright 2018

Conscious Commentary Publishing LLC
BUY Born Free's books from Amazon.com
linktr.ee/therealbornfree

Dedication

This book is dedicated to the Creator (YAH),
our Ancestors, my Parents, Pauline Ramsey,
Safiya, YennnnnnA (you're a great mom!),
Mrs. Stubbs, Mrs. Johnson, Crystal Brown,
and to everyone who woke up this morning!!!

Acknowledgements

Thank you, Almighty YAH, our Ancestors, Safiya, Nima, Wallace Ford, MO, Kush, John Robinson, and my Intelligent Muzik family for helping me pull this project together and keeping me on track and focused. I know I can drag my feet and procrastinate, so I'm incredibly appreciative and grateful that y'all stayed with me for the full ride!

Morning Wake Up Calls – Born Free

for Safiya
#buddypals4life

Introduction

Good morning Beloved. I pray that you slept well. It's never easy jumping right up and getting into the life and death struggle of achieving our goals and dreams. There's always the temptation, the seduction, the desire to get a few more seconds of precious sleep – to hit that heavenly snooze button at least 3 more times before we even turn over once. That glorious new sunlight that is pushing past our tightly drawn curtains and attacking our unsuspecting eyelids with the promise of today's new possibilities, can be terrifying and dreadful. Trust me, I understand this feeling all too well.

I know it's much easier to stay in the cool darkness and snuggle 93 million miles under a mountain of soft, warm, thick, and cozy comforters, then to get up and deal with the truth of the new day. The horror of waking up suddenly only to realize that 8 fantastic hours of freedom flew by in the blink of your sleepy eyes is often frightening, and more times than not, you've chosen to deal with a torrent of scary nightmares over waking up and dealing with your current reality. Believe me, I've been there many-many times. Those feelings are extremely human and normal. It's completely natural to desire to sink deep into the dreamy abyss of sleep's forgetfulness. But beloved, we must break free from the addiction and distractions of over-sleeping, nostalgic dreams, denial, excuses, fear of failure, anxiety, lies, escapism, gossip, talking and texting, mindlessly scrolling through social media, and all the other bullshit that trips us up. The first step is by getting the fuck out of our beds and doing exactly what we know needs to be done to achieve our hearts desires. You know I'm right! Come on let's go, you got this!

The main purpose of these **Morning Wake Up Calls** is to get your thoughts, intentions, and actions in alignment with the infinite power of creation. To become one with God. To connect with the creative principle that exists in all things. That supreme and dynamic force of nature that abides in our hearts but is buried under years of self-destructive miseducation and misdirection. Look around you and bear witness to life's diverse abundance.

Look inside yourself and feel the God given power surging through every fiber of your being. It's always there. It's always been there. I know you can feel it. I know you want to unleash it. You are limitless in your capacity. You can manifest whatever you can conceive. The only caveat is, belief! For these **Morning Wake Up Calls** to work, **YOU MUST BELIEVE IN YOURSELF! FUCK fear!** You **MUST** block out all the **HATE** and **DISTRACTIONS!** You **CAN'T** let anything, or anybody get in your **WAY!** I know it's been overstated and an old cliché', but you must **SEIZE THE TIME!**

Your success and abundance depend on your unshakeable belief in self. You must be willing to fight for YOU! Yes, everything that I just said is easier said than done. I struggle daily with the same damn things, but at some point, all roads will lead back to "Fuck it, just do it!" Eventually, you will have to put it all on the line. **Do or Die!** And the best time to get into this **ACTION FRAME OF MIND** is as soon as you get up in the morning. Before you open your eyes start telling yourself that today you're going to get everything that you need, want, and deserve. Tell yourself that you will begin controlling your life.

Today, make a firm and clear declaration that you won't let anybody, or anything get in your way. Enough is enough! Today take all those ideas, thoughts, and inventions off the shelf and set them loose on the world. I know it's exhausting watching other people cross the finish lines of their lives while you're on the sidelines clicking like on their social media platforms. It's time for you to show and prove your love and devotion through your ways and actions.

These **Morning Wake Up Calls** will remind you of what you already know down deep in your heart of hearts. They are specifically designed to keep you in that action mindset. If you don't put these Wake Up Calls into motion, you will NOT achieve anything or go anywhere! Knowledge is power, but action is the rapture! You have the power in your hands to do whatever you want to do. Only you can stop you!

Know and understand that waking up today is your first major victory in your ongoing battle for mental, physical, spiritual, emotional, and financial success. It's the first thing that must happen for you to change the landscape and course of your life. Yes, waking up is a big fucking deal. Be extremely grateful because millions of people around the globe aren't as fortunate as you are right now. Waking up places you back in the game and gives you another chance to finish what you started. So, please don't take being alive for granted because it's not guaranteed that tomorrow will be available to you. The next crucial step is fixing your mind's eye on the north star of positivity and possibility. Coming of age, I was taught an acronym for the word peace: **P**ositive **E**nergy **A**ctivates **C**onstant **E**levation. This major key helped me focus my thoughts and energy on keeping negativity away from me. Keeping negative, unmotivated, dreamless, and visionless people away from you is vital for your success.

It sounds like a simple no brainer, but so many of us stumble at this extremely critical juncture at the beginning of our day. We keep inviting the same people that consistently bring us down and hold us back- back into our lives every day. I'm not suggesting that you randomly start ghosting your friends and family for no damn reason. You know what I'm saying, and you know who I'm talking about! I'm referring to those people who don't add anything of true value to you or your life's mission. You know, the takers. The folks who just withdraw from your accounts and never invest in them. The ones who only call you with problems and never have any real solutions. The people who manifest this negative, immature, jealous, envious, and hateful spiritual energy, must be removed from your cipher immediately. Don't underestimate the power of the dark side of the force! Please take this jewel seriously.

The next thing you must do is stop wringing your hands over your past mistakes and missed opportunities. We all get caught up in a sickening loop of regressive and negative "coulda, woulda, shoulda's" and lay uncomfortably in our beds replaying our mistakes, missteps, and indiscretions endlessly. We regurgitate our problems and issues until we choke on them; and far too often, this becomes our norm and we carry this motionless stench around with us for the rest of our lives. Don't let yesterday's setbacks and disappointments cloud the new day's sky and obscure the brilliance of all the new and exciting opportunities that you have right within your grasp. We all have fucked up! We all have made some serious errors of judgment. Please forgive yourself and get the fuck back up! It's not over Beloved! As long as you're alive you have a chance to make it happen for yourself. As you read and heed these **Morning Wake Up Calls**, great things will start unfolding for you. After you read them to yourself, say them out loud, and then put them in motion!

None of these affirmations will tell you that if you close your eyes and say I'm a millionaire, you'll magically become a millionaire. That's bullshit and manipulative! Hard work is mandatory! It's no getting around that fact. Everything written in this book was created to get you focused and ready to manifest your infinite possibilities in the real world. To get the most out of this book, you must stay in the **ACTION FRAME OF MIND**. That action frame of mind is indispensable to this process of mental, spiritual, physical, and financial resurrection.

I also must add that when you start down the path of loving yourself, accepting yourself, caring about yourself, being happy with yourself, and fighting for your dreams, you will face major difficulties. You will face some major opposition from those who benefit from your current state and position. Get ready to have some very uncomfortable and hard conversations with the people in your life who don't want you to change for the better. Just take a deep breath, you're going to be okay. Change is always scary. Transformation and rebirth can be painful, but it's necessary to be truly successful and happy.

Everything written in these pages is to help you get motivated and active in the pursuit of your happiness. I want you to know how wonderful you are and how the rest of the world is a better place because you're alive. You are a unique and beautiful expression of God's mercy and grace. Let go of all the self-doubt and disbelief. You have a powerful story to tell, and the world is waiting to hear it.

You must do something positive and constructive with your life. You must bring something of value and substance into physical existence. Remember, knowledge is power, but **ACTION** is the rapture! Now let's go! Good Morning Beloved! This is your Morning Wake Up Call. Get the hell up! Pray, focus, get refined, get dressed, get something healthy to eat, and command your thoughts and actions to get out in the world and make your mark! **TODAY IS THE DAY!**

Born Free #therealbornfree

**before the moment you open your eyes
choices are being made
you must decide if you're going to ride
in the funeral procession or in life's parade**

(Wake Up Call #1)

Good Morning
take a second to be grateful
reject the hateful
throw off useless labels
be faithful and thankful
you made it to this moment
life's sublime
hit the ground running
and seize the time

∞

(Wake Up Call #2)

Good Morning
hit the sky flying
it's so gratifying
grab all your theories
and start applying
I know climbing to new heights
can be terrifying
but success lives and gives
on the horizon of dying

∞

(Wake Up Call #3)

Good Morning
be mindful of who you let
whisper in your ear

∞

(Wake Up Call #4)

Good Morning
no more speculation
make a clear declaration
no stagnation
rise above all expectations
breakdown every wall
break through every ceiling
and once you open your heart to healing
you'll be victorious in all your dealings

∞

(Wake Up Call #5)

Good Morning
don't exhaust your resources
on frivolous things
cut yourself loose
from materialistic strings
travel light
you don't need the extra baggage
chasing what the world views as lavish
can cause your fortune to vanish

∞

(Wake Up Call #6)

Good Morning
seek power
first inner, then outer
without it
you and yours will be devoured

∞

(Wake Up Call #7)

Good Morning
without physical power
you can't win an earthly war
prayers alone won't stop them
from kicking down your door

∞

(Wake Up Call #8)

Good Morning
don't get distracted by images
trust your gut

∞

(Wake Up Call #9)

Good Morning
set your intentions
no more apprehensions
your dreams aren't bound
by this dimension
take a deep breath
discipline your steps
this world hasn't seen
the best of you yet

∞

(Wake Up Call #10)

Good Morning
you can't give a fuck
if nobody believes in your ideas
you can't give a fuck
if your closest friends start to disappear
I know it's not fair
I know that shit hurts
but if you give up your dreams for them
you'll feel even worse

(Wake Up Call #11)

Good Morning
change your environment
travel outside your comfort zone
go somewhere unknown
don't be afraid to take a journey alone
be a pioneer
go beyond the frontier
the wealthy
make major moves despite their fears

∞

(Wake Up Call #12)

Good Morning
wake the fuck up!
start the revolution
we already know the problem
be the solution
come to the conclusion
to expose the illusion
no more vain showin'
it's time to start provin'

∞

(Wake Up Call #13)

Good Morning
time for a mind state switch
adjust your pitch
elevate your thinking
if you want to get rich
get your priorities in order
put away childish things
spread your wings
and you'll be one of the
prosperous Queens and Kings

∞

(Wake Up Call #14)

Good Morning
your demons are always lurkin'
seducin' and flirtin'
know this for certain
the devil is always workin'
negativity always goes viral
whether it's homicidal or suicidal
spiritually prepare for its arrival
faith and prayer are vital for your survival

∞

(Wake Up Call #15)

Good Morning
success and greatness
isn't measured by possessions
money isn't a synonym
for heaven
success and greatness
comes from living your best life
being your natural self
is your God given birthright
don't let anybody define you
by the size of your wallet
that's false knowledge
your success and greatness
doesn't live in your pocket
your supreme and divine power
comes from your mind, soul, and heart
if you're looking for success and greatness
that's where you should start

∞

(Wake Up Call #16)

Good Morning
stop being afraid of them
and start making them afraid of you!

∞

(Wake Up Call #17)

Good Morning
be mindful beloved,
you don't have to hate them
for them to hate you
you don't have to lie on them
for them to lie on you
you don't have to plot against them
for them to plot against you
and you don't have to hurt them
for them to try and hurt you
BE AWARE!

∞

(Wake Up Call #18)

Good Morning
stay VIGILANT
tune your INSTRUMENT
side-step the INSIGNIFICANT
blow past the BELLIGERENT
ignore the IGNORANT
teach the ILLITERATE
protect the INNOCENT
embrace the OMNIPOTENT

∞

(Wake Up Call #19)

Good Morning
nobody's life is easy
don't get lost in your losses
stay focused and honest
no plan is flawless
don't get nauseous
or too exhausted
these are the stepping-stones
of bosses

∞

(Wake Up Call #20)

Good Morning
radiate positive vibrations
anticipate complications
don't run from confrontations
fortify your foundation
stay inspired
make your only direction higher
remove all negative people
from your cipher

∞

(Wake Up Call #21)

Good Morning
have the balls to be you!

∞

(Wake Up Call #22)

Good Morning
if you don't rise above it
you'll fall backward and become it

∞

(Wake Up Call #23)

Good Morning
don't take the best of you to the graveyard
exhaust as many of God's gifts as possible
don't take the best of you to the graveyard
wasting your abundance is unconscionable
don't take the best of you to the graveyard
share what God shared with you
don't take the best of you to the graveyard
ignored blessings don't accrue

∞

(Wake Up Call #24)

Good Morning
push past yesterday's setbacks
get off the mat
get on track
go on the attack
getting knocked down
is a part of a champions path
be steadfast
you'll have the last laugh

∞

(Wake Up Call #25)

Good Morning
get your money
it's a human necessity
it can help you escape poverty
but don't sacrifice your integrity
because without your humanity
your money is worthless
it loses all purpose
it's unworthy of your worship

∞

(Wake Up Call #26)

Good Morning
that million dollars
just won't fall in your lap
if you believe otherwise
you've fallen into the media's trap
everything of value
must be worked for and earned
this is the true get money lesson
that must be learned

(Wake Up Call #27)

Good Morning
don't be intimidated by the game
set fire to the flame
grab your flag
and stake your claim
lead the charge
dominate the discourse
have a determined idea
and move with a determined force

∞

(Wake Up Call #28)

Good Morning
no more talking
no more squawking
if you're not going to do it
start fuckin' walking
no more bullshit
no more fallacies
it's time to make
your rhetoric your reality

∞

(Wake Up Call #29)

Good Morning
GET UP EARLY
and STAY in the
ACTION FRAME OF MIND

∞

(Wake Up Call #30)

Good Morning
pick your battles
don't get caught in trivial pursuits
save your ammo
only shoot when it's time to shoot
don't allow yourself to be baited
don't get maneuvered out of position
walk away from anything
that takes you away
from your life's mission

∞

(Wake Up Call #31)

Good Morning
FUCK THE ODDS!

∞

(Wake Up Call #32)

Good Morning
don't let other people
use your ambition against you

∞

(Wake Up Call #33)

Good Morning
the truth is not a suggestion
don't let lies seep into your organization
truly successful people
honor their obligations
their word is their bond
their bond is their life
deceit will diminish and extinguish
your God given light

∞

(Wake Up Call #34)

Good Morning
let the force of God awaken you
let the force of God penetrate you
let the force of God stimulate you
let the force of God embolden you
let the force of God fortify you
let the force of God guide you
let the force of God surprise you
let the force of God revive you

∞

(Wake Up Call #35)

Good Morning
pick your team wisely
understand their psyche
don't take this lightly
or make your choice blindly
no one can do it alone
you need a strong support system
your network will make
you the victor or the victim

∞

(Wake Up Call #36)

Good Morning
it's **NOT** about
how much you have
it's about
what you do with what you have
let me repeat that again
it's **NOT** about
how much you have
it's about
what you do with what you have

∞

(Wake Up Call #37)

Good Morning
each second that you sit there
another great opportunity is lost
get back into the mix
before you incur another loss
get saddled with another bill
be forced to climb another hill
you have the talents and skills
but do you have courage, heart, and will?

∞

(Wake Up Call #38)

Good Morning
everything is right within your grasp
the mystery is about to be unmasked
you started off strong
but you must finish the task
don't fall back
or celebrate too fast
cross the finish line
before you take a victory lap

∞

(Wake Up Call #39)

Good Morning
don't give in
to those dark thoughts
don't forget the good lessons
you were taught
it's not over
you're not finished
this is just another scrimmage
it's okay to go get replenished
it's normal to ask questions
it's normal to feel the tension
but don't let anything
stop your forward progression
it's normal to feel sadness
it's normal to want to pause
but you must find the inner strength
to bear your cross

∞

(Wake Up Call #40)

Good Morning
you won't reach your destination
if you're moving half ass
giving up now
is worst then coming in last
coming in last
means that you had the will power
to finish the race
but if you quit now
your legacy will be erased

∞

(Wake Up Call #41)

Good Morning
don't tell negative people
about your plans and dreams
they'll immediately start working
on breaking down your self-esteem
they have nothing going for themselves
so, they have the time to hate on you
stay focused on your goals
and keep doing what
God created you to do

∞

(Wake Up Call #42)

Good Morning
transformation isn't easy
and that's a good thing
not many people
can survive this fiery ring
but you can
you can push all the pain aside
get into your stride
and stand where champions reside
I have no doubt in my mind
that you're a natural born winner
because you've never been
or will ever be
a coward or a quitter

∞

(Wake Up Call #43)

Good Morning
develop a pattern for victory
nothing will happen randomly
manifest your best daily
and you'll move closer to your destiny

∞

(Wake Up Call #44)

Good Morning
growth is supposed to hurt

∞

(Wake Up Call #45)

Good Morning
you have my permission and blessing
to do whatever you have to do
to get back home safely and unharmed

∞

(Wake Up Call #46)

Good Morning
make, remake,
and break the rules constantly
EVOLVE!!!

∞

(Wake Up Call #47)

Good Morning
offense, offense, offense

∞

(Wake Up Call #48)

Good Morning
fight the urge to be mediocre
fight the urge to be ordinary
fight the urge to be invisible
fight the urge to be contrary
you were born excellent
God blessed you from the start
now step out of the dark
and set yourself a part!

∞

(Wake Up Call #49)

Good Morning
engage the world as it is
and not how you wish it to be
that's the only way
to change fucked up realities
if you choose to ignore harsh truths
because you're afraid of the repercussions
all your private big talk
will publicly amount to nothing

∞

(Wake Up Call #50)

Good Morning
stay hungry!
a full belly slows you down
and makes you sleepy

∞

(Wake Up Call #51)

Good Morning
empower yourself
energize yourself
enable yourself
enfranchise yourself
enrich yourself
equip yourself
enhearten yourself
educate yourself
encourage yourself
establish yourself
enlighten yourself
emancipate yourself

∞

(Wake Up Call #52)

Good Morning
don't hit the snooze
spark the fuse
go make some moves
start making the news
give this world something new
to discuss and debate
declare yourself
the master of your fate

∞

(Wake Up Call #53)

Good Morning
action and inaction changes everything

∞

(Wake Up Call #54)

Good Morning
don't be afraid to be different
a new batch or mismatched
the irregular thinker
is impossible to catch
embrace your uniqueness
it will put you at the front of the pack
always remember
if you're not a little bit weird
you're all the way wack

∞

(Wake Up Call #55)

Good Morning
be humble
but not to the point
where you give the next person
an advantage over you

∞

(Wake Up Call #56)

Good Morning
we all get disappointed
we all get depressed
we all get hit hard
we all get stressed
but the true warrior
uses all that negative force
to put them back on the horse
and keep them right on course

∞

(Wake Up Call #57)

Good Morning
don't just go along to get along
or blindly sing the company's work songs
don't confuse right and wrong
this is how they spiritually kill the strong
they want your compliance
they need your silence
don't confuse lambs with lions
and don't be quiet
BE DEFIANT!

∞

(Wake Up Call #58)

Good Morning
get up earlier than everybody else
stay later than everybody else
be more dedicated than everybody else
be more focused than everybody else
be more faithful than everybody else
be more resolute than everybody else
ask more questions than everybody else
train harder than everybody else

(Wake Up Call #59)

Good Morning
stop the endless debates
give us a break
it's time to create
your life can't wait
if you don't stop talking shit
verbally going around and around
your seeds will stay stuck
dying underground

∞

(Wake Up Call #60)

Good Morning
let the old anger go
let the freshwater flow
the extra emotional weight
is why you're moving so slow
I know I'm from the outside
and it's easier said than done
but if you've only loaded your gun
those assholes from your past have won

∞

(Wake Up Call #61)

Good Morning
don't hold on to your grudges for too long
they might not ever let you go

∞

(Wake Up Call #62)

Good Morning
don't confuse real power
with regulated and controlled access

∞

(Wake Up Call #63)

Good Morning
the leaders that you voted for
are **NOT** the true leaders of the country
NEVER forget that

∞

(Wake Up Call #64)

Good Morning
don't put politicians
in the savior position
voting every few years
won't make them listen
they'll never do for you
what you must do for yourself
they'll never go against their backers
to give you any meaningful help

∞

(Wake Up Call #65)

Good Morning
I know the news can be heartbreaking
white supremacist mass shootings
red and blue death-banging
left and right prostituting
it's all revolting
sickening
the wickedness
we're witnessing
but no matter how disheartening
no matter how much you're appalled
the only way for things to change
is for people of good conscious
to get involved

∞

(Wake Up Call #66)

Good Morning
always fight for self-sufficiency
human dignity
moral consistency
and spiritual symmetry
avoid ignorant mimicry
false religious imagery
and **NEVER** sell your divinity
to be a part of the devil's industry

∞

(Wake Up Call #67)

Good Morning
be a myth-buster
be an instructor
be a constructor
be a hunter
be a risk taker
be a creator
be major
be a force of nature

∞

(Wake Up Call #68)

Good Morning
use what you have
to get what you need and want
you don't need a ton of money
to start your hunt
having less can give you an advantage
it makes you more creative
it makes you more flexible
innovative and asymmetrical

∞

(Wake Up Call #69)

Good Morning
get your mental and physical health
in alignment
understand
it's supreme power in refinement
life and death
lives in your diet
study the science of food
understand your body's requirements
all things in moderation
we speak through vibrations
it's time to evolve past
the menu from the plantation
real soul food
heals your divine spirit
illuminates your appearance
and makes everything in existence
crystal clear and vivid

∞

(Wake Up Call #70)

Good Morning
be proactive
cause some static and havoc
you can't reach the masses
if you're acting passive
be explosive
devoted and ferocious
balance intellect with emotion
be as open as the ocean

∞

(Wake Up Call #71)

Good Morning
get out of bed
forget the dread
purge the procrastination
from your heart and head
set some meetings
refocus your vision
bust out of
self-doubts prison

∞

(Wake Up Call #72)

Good Morning
stop fucking complaining
and over explaining
only you
can stop it from raining
use these fucked up moments
to build up your resolve
don't leave the mysteries of your life
uninvestigated and unsolved

∞

(Wake Up Call #73)

Good Morning
fight through the misery
fight through the painful history
fight through the afflictions
fight through the addictions
fight through the suicidal urge
fight through the hateful words
fight through the rejections
fight through the oppression

(Wake Up Call #74)

Good Morning
the same people
that you start your journey with
are **NOT** necessarily the same people
you'll end it with
get ready
be prepared
and continue to grow
no matter what happens next

∞

(Wake Up Call #75)

Good Morning
ignorance, apathy, and laziness
are contagious!
stay away from people
who have these spiritual diseases

∞

(Wake Up Call #76)

Good Morning
break the trance
you've been given another chance
to complete your life's work
evolve, advance
rejoin the dance
love, grow, and shine
the worst thing you could do today
is waste your time

∞

(Wake Up Call #77)

Good Morning
don't be mundane
or just passable
go against the grain
be magical
don't be satisfactory
or forgettable
be extraordinary
be formidable

∞

(Wake Up Call #78)

Good Morning
never fail in the wrong direction
whenever you fail
make sure that you fail forward

∞

(Wake Up Call #79)

Good Morning
before you jump up to work and play
kneel and pray
let God help you
define your agenda for the day
your faith will breed success
be determined to get your wealth
the doubters don't matter
as long as you believe in yourself

∞

(Wake Up Call #80)

Good Morning
God gave you life
God gave you the talent
God gave you the ability
to conquer any challenge
God gave you your gifts
God gave you these lessons
God wants you to understand
that your entire journey is a blessing

∞

(Wake Up Call #81)

Good Morning
do more
love more
give more
listen more
achieve more
participate more
create more
communicate more
innovate more
speak up more
connect more
bless more
read more
think more
grow more
pray more

∞

(Wake Up Call #82)

Good Morning
be forgiving
be compassionate
be understanding
be honest
be empathetic
be non-judgmental
be introspective
be thoughtful
be gentle
be human
be considerate
be literate
be endearing
be grateful
be friendly
be neighborly

∞

(Wake Up Call #83)

Good Morning
time is not forever
when you're dealing with the flesh
you can rest
but always stay dressed
hold sacred every breath
hasten your steps, progress
empty your soul out
before God introduces you to death

∞

(Wake Up Call #84)

Good Morning
winners have an abundance of
courage, conviction,
compassion, and character

∞

(Wake Up Call #85)

Good Morning
ambition doesn't wait for permission
forget the audition and competition
turn the key in the ignition
start on your mission
redefine the definitions
write your own compositions
don't do for public recognition
do it because it's your passion and vision

(Wake Up Call #86)

Good Morning
don't wait for the next person to do it
step up and do it yourself
don't wait for the next person to suggest it
step up and suggest it yourself
don't wait for approval
lead the next generation of women and men
patience is a virtue
but wasting time is a sin

∞

(Wake Up Call #87)

Good Morning
don't wait for the alarm to sound
before you make your move

∞

(Wake Up Call #88)

Good Morning
get out of your own way
don't lead yourself astray
stop contradicting
everything you do and say
your excuses and anxiety
are tripping you up tremendously
please don't be
your own worst enemy

∞

(Wake Up Call #89)

Good Morning
keep your standards high
place them above the sky
the second you lower them
real opportunities pass by
I know it feels easier and faster
it might bring you a little joy and laughter
but lowering yourself and your standards
is ultimately a disaster

(Wake Up Call #90)

Good Morning
if you can't trust them
DON'T try to love them

∞

(Wake Up Call #91)

Good Morning
whenever you strike
make sure that you strike
with a blinding force

∞

(Wake Up Call #92)

Good Morning
every thought
isn't meant to be spoken out loud
or posted online

∞

(Wake Up Call #93)

Good Morning
always put God first
always put his word first
because when we don't
we make a home inside a hearse
when God is the standard
in our personal and business affairs
we feel the love everywhere
and we're free
from destruction and despair

∞

(Wake Up Call #94)

Good Morning
always put family first
always put your children first
don't sacrifice your home
to satisfy your corporate thirsts
remember the reason
you embarked on your financial endeavor
worldly fortune could never
compare to familial treasures

∞

(Wake Up Call #95)

Good Morning
stop over analyzing
revising and revising
you can't foresee everything
so please stop trying
perfection isn't required
free your mind
just do your fuckin' best
and stay on your grind

∞

(Wake Up Call #96)

Good Morning
stop arguing with fools
fools love being fools
it's a waste of energy
don't play by their rules
people without goals
and festering holes in their souls
will consciously or unconsciously
run you off the road

∞

(Wake Up Call #97)

Good Morning
today is about loving yourself
today is about understanding yourself
it's about looking within
and appreciating your true wealth
do something that makes you happy
you're abundantly alive
you deserve this
you shall not be denied

∞

(Wake Up Call #98)

Good Morning
today is the day that you get a grip
and refuse to slip
today is the day that you give up
all toxic relationships
don't allow anybody
to use or abuse you
don't allow anybody
to violate or hurt you
you're a child of God
a child of the light
kick them out of your life
if they can't love and treat you right

∞

(Wake Up Call #99)

Good Morning
take pride in your accomplishments
have supreme confidence
look in the mirror and give yourself
a much-deserved compliment
be proud of yourself
you've come a long-long way
get dressed
and walk at the head of the parade today

(Wake Up Call #100)

Good Morning
today is about accountability
transparency
dependability
and creditability
this is the currency
that comes from living with integrity
which far exceeds
anything that you could acquire monetarily

∞

(Wake Up Call #101)

Good Morning
it's normal to have regrets
confess and God will lift your stress
what happened-happened
make amends, take new steps
lift your head up
make the most of your new situation
don't let guilt stop you
from arriving at a better destination

(Wake Up Call #102)

Good Morning
tweeting about it
isn't enough
posting pictures about it
isn't enough
sharing videos about it
isn't enough
reading this book
isn't enough
don't confuse
online #hastagism
with real world
activism
if your boots aren't tightly laced
and moving forcefully forward on the ground
quite frankly beloved,
you're just bullshittin' around

∞

(Wake Up Call #103)

Good Morning
pain is always a part of the process
pain always knows your home address
but don't bow down and acquiesce
or run away and regress
the pain is making you stronger
the pain is making you last longer
the pain is giving you the ultimate power
to grow and flower

∞

(Wake Up Call #104)

Good Morning
put a smile on your face
prepare to be embraced
a positive attitude
can blast you straight into space
BE HAPPY
let the world see those pearly whites
BE HAPPY
let the world see your magnificent light
I know it's hard to summon a smile
when the world is on your shoulders
but the fire inside a smile
can help you feel a little less colder

∞

(Wake Up Call #105)

Good Morning
take your gears off cruise
don't be confused
if you're not enthused
nobody else is going to be enthused
if you're not hype about you
why should anybody else
don't expect them to believe in you
if you don't even believe in yourself

∞

(Wake Up Call #106)

Good Morning
find the fortune in the fad
the good in the bad
look for the lessons
don't waste precious seconds being mad
unexpected things arise
study each obstacle
discover what is possible
and become unstoppable

(Wake Up Call #107)

Good Morning
the European slave trade wasn't our choice
separate the real from the false voice
avoid the convoys of employed decoys
sent to exploit, distract, and, destroy
these walking dead talking heads
put poison in clickbait threads
but if you remember what God said
their sickness won't spread

∞

(Wake Up Call #108)

Good Morning
don't be a slave
don't be a nigger/nigga
don't be an idiot
don't be corny
don't be a coward
don't be stupid
don't be a chump
because all the above
nobody wants

∞

(Wake Up Call #109)

Good Morning
don't be a clown
don't be fake
don't be uninformed
don't be the norm
don't be a jackass
don't be a little bitch
don't be puppet
because all the above
nobody wants it

∞

(Wake Up Call #110)

Good Morning
don't be a sucka
don't be a wack mother fucka
don't be a loser
don't be an abuser
don't be a dickhead
don't be a cunt
don't be like Trump
because all the above
nobody wants

∞

(Wake Up Call #111)

Good Morning
don't be a thief
don't be a creep
don't be a sneak
don't be a sheep
don't be a biter
don't be a stunt
please-please don't be like Trump
because all the above
nobody wants

∞

(Wake Up Call #112)

Good Morning
be invincible
be earth shattering
let these slave masters know
that you're not the one for capturing
be victorious
be notorious
and no matter what you do
be Vanglorious

∞

(Wake Up Call #113)

Good Morning
be admirable
be astute
be the person
that the whole world salutes
be upstanding
be commanding
be the brand
that every company calls for branding

∞

(Wake Up Call #114)

Good Morning
be honorable
don't be miserable
be the one
that makes the comfortable uncomfortable
be brave
be the rave
don't be the rider
be the wave

∞

(Wake Up Call #115)

Good Morning
be the brainchild
be the new style
be the one
that drives all the haters wild
be the new movement
be the visionary
be the futurist
that everyone thinks is crazy

∞

(Wake Up Call #116)

Good Morning
amazing things
are happening right now
don't over question the why
or be suspicious of the how
you're finally moving forward
with your goals and plans
you finally put your life
back in your capable hands

(Wake Up Call #117)

Good Morning
you've entered a new phase
the sun is ablaze
you finally found your way
out this serpentine maze
it took a while
a lot of jewels were learned
your days on the sidelines are over
it's your turn to burn

∞

(Wake Up Call #118)

Good Morning
invest in your community
uplift your community
build with you neighbors
connect with them truthfully
grow beyond self-satisfaction
selfish interactions
because without a unified action
all you get are impotent reactions

∞

(Wake Up Call #119)

Good Morning
embrace the fullness of life
embrace the glory of life
embrace the full power of love
climb to new heights
embrace your true self
embrace your possibilities
embrace the reality
of God's infinite capacity

∞

(Wake Up Call #120)

Good Morning
you're greater than your greatest mistake
don't succumb to the hate
God will never turn away
his forgiving face
don't let fake people
chain you to your worse moment
make your atonement
move on and own it

∞

(Wake Up Call #121)

Good Morning
release your limitless power
turn away from the doubters
let your love and actions
speak louder
believe in yourself
come out of your shell
open your heart
you have a great story to tell

∞

(Wake Up Call #122)

Good Morning
be courageous
have faith and patience
dreams are ageless
don't focus on becoming famous
or the up and down
changes and stages
this journey isn't painless
but the divine struggle
is the path to greatness

∞

(Wake Up Call #123)

Good Morning
your unwavering belief in yourself
and your unbreakable self-confidence
is worth more
than all your money in the bank

∞

(Wake Up Call #124)

Good Morning
don't let your unwavering belief in yourself
and your unbreakable self-confidence
mutate into grotesque arrogance
and reckless cockiness
narcissistic ignorance
cynical callousness
hypocritical laziness
and self-destructive obnoxiousness

∞

(Wake Up Call #125)

Good Morning
create your own business model
make new footprints to follow
be the hero
in your own novel

∞

(Wake Up Call #126)

Good Morning
think global
take your marketing plan to foreign lands
set up trading posts
constantly evolve yourself and your brand
create new shipping lanes
open new veins
if you're not trying to dominate the game
you're going to get pushed out the frame

∞

(Wake Up Call #127)

Good Morning
once you stop learning and growing
it's over

∞

(Wake Up Call #128)

Good Morning
go hard
and right when you think you're done
go even harder

∞

(Wake Up Call #129)

Good Morning
don't fuck people over
and don't let people fuck you over

∞

(Wake Up Call #130)

Good Morning
stop living like you're in mourning
it's not rewarding
it's boring
stop letting others do all the scoring
put on your shoes
hit the street
get back in the game
it's time to compete

∞

(Wake Up Call #131)

Good Morning
you don't have to choose between
your sexual side
your intellectual side
your emotional side
or your spiritual side
combine them
into one powerful expression
and shine that brilliant light
across this world and beyond

∞

(Wake Up Call #132)

Good Morning
don't forget to openly love
and take care of yourself today

∞

(Wake Up Call #133)

Good Morning
your discipline
will dictate your direction
your ascension will be based
on wherever you place your attention
push yourself
don't choose the lighter load
unopened gifts
will erode and implode

∞

(Wake Up Call #134)

Good Morning
it's okay to take a few steps back
discard old bootstraps
rethink, reload
relook at your map
adjustments are normal
in fact, it's a must
real life will never be exactly like
what was dreamed about and discussed

∞

(Wake Up Call #135)

Good Morning
don't ever struggle to be second
or an also ran
if you're not trying to be the best
you're not the right woman or man
if you're not trying to have your wingspan
eclipse the stars, moon, and sun
hang it up beloved
you're already done

∞

(Wake Up Call #136)

Good Morning
stay away from distractions
and dysfunction
never participate
in your own destruction
the devil is always baiting
the sunken place is always waiting
so, whenever you're operating
make sure that you're
righteously navigating

∞

(Wake Up Call #137)

Good Morning
stop playing the background
don't co-sign the village idiot and clown
stop sleep walking through life
without making a sound
make your presence known
don't postpone
carve your legacy
in stone, flesh, and bone

∞

(Wake Up Call #138)

Good Morning
hustle hard
but hustle smart
hustle from the soul
hustle from your heart
hustle or get hustled
and all hustles aren't illegal
cuz when you hustle with a divine purpose
your hustle elevates all people

∞

(Wake Up Call #139)

Good Morning
study your physical environment
master your spiritual environment
balancing all your elements
will bring you the greatest benefits
you'll never be defeated
once you master
your inner and outer terrain
you'll be able
to find happiness
in the center of the hurricane

∞

(Wake Up Call #140)

Good Morning
if you truly want it
you'll have to fight for it
claw, scratch
and bite for it
workday and night
for it
give and take
a life for it
if you truly want it
if you truly need to have it
you need to be
as committed as an addict

∞

(Wake Up Call #141)

Good Morning
be tenacious
be audacious
be adventurous
be outrageous
be inventive
be inquisitive
be enterprising
be surprising
be dauntless
be rapturous
be the dissident
be a maverick
be whimsical
be unconventional
be scholastic
be iconoclastic

∞

(Wake Up Call #142)

Good Morning
the person next to you in bed
the person that you choose to wed
needs to be in alignment
with the dreams in your heart and head
they must be more
that just your sexual partner
a sweet charmer
they must actively work
to help take the best of you farther

∞

(Wake Up Call #143)

Good Morning
if your relationship is abusive and toxic,
DROP IT!

∞

(Wake Up Call #144)

Good Morning
if they didn't help you till the field
don't let them help you eat the meal

∞

(Wake Up Call #145)

Good Morning
if you don't know about the subject
being talked about and addressed
keep your damn mouth closed
until you research and assess
speaking prematurely
or before you completely understand
will undermine your personal reputation
and severely weaken your brand

∞

(Wake Up Call #146)

Good Morning
renew your history
reaffirm your vows
it isn't about what you did then
it's about what you're doing now
life's dynamic
positive energy activates constant elevation
your trains must always be
leaving the station

∞

(Wake Up Call #147)

Good Morning
never water down your brand
never sully your reputation
never treat honesty and sincerity
as mere decoration
everything that you do
will announce you in advance
your reputation is what gets you
those life changing connections and contacts

∞

(Wake Up Call #148)

Good Morning
sometimes you have to say fuck it
sometimes you have to say fuck you
most times you have to do
some shit that you don't want to do
because silver trays don't exist
overnight success is a myth
you gotta go beyond your limits
to get life's most precious gifts

∞

(Wake Up Call #149)

Good Morning
once you begin to feel entitled
you begin to lose everything

∞

(Wake Up Call #150)

Good Morning
everybody hits a wall
everybody takes more than a few on the chin
everybody struggles with
how and when to begin
please don't beat yourself up
if your intro to the world is a little shaky
don't worry about getting
all the lumps out of your gravy
just start doing
start pursuing
you can work out all the kinks later
JUST START MOVING!

∞

(Wake Up Call #151)

Good Morning
giving up is not an option
no stopping
no plodding
opportunity won't keep knocking
no matter who's blocking
run right through them
and it doesn't matter who they send
your worst enemy or your best friend

∞

(Wake Up Call #152)

Good Morning
you can't wait for help to come
it might not get there in enough time
you can't wait to hook up the safety line
before you start your climb
you gotta go now
you gotta risk it all
you gotta go into it knowing
that you're probably going to fall
but you can't let that stop you
welcome your failures with open arms
because it's inaction and not failure
that brings you the most harm

∞

(Wake Up Call #153)

Good Morning
it only matters if you do something about it

∞

(Wake Up Call #154)

Good Morning
when you fuck up
admit it
own it
don't make excuses
expose it
this is how you grow
this is how you maintain prosperity
transparency
is how you keep your
integrity and authority

∞

(Wake Up Call #155)

Good Morning
don't be romanced by happenstance
and no money down finance
don't follow folly
or get caught up in the lottery of chance
put your money on you
on the power of your assured will
the only bet you should take
is on your own skills

∞

(Wake Up Call #156)

Good Morning
don't play the blame game
because nobody's cares
accept the fact
that life will never be fair
but that's okay
you're going to make it regardless
you're going to work the smartest
and reap the full bounty
of the harvest

∞

(Wake Up Call #157)

Good Morning
victory is going to ask you to sacrifice
more than you can imagine

∞

(Wake Up Call #158)

Good Morning
if you need help, ask for it
but DON'T become addicted to it

(Wake Up Call #159)

Good Morning
create your own future
create your own lane
create your own excitement
create your own fame
create your own history
create your own legacy
create your own philosophy
create your own reality

∞

(Wake Up Call #160)

Good Morning
write your own rules
use your own tools
and never confuse
horses with mules
study more jewels
build and teach at your own schools
and never waste time
suffering fools

∞

(Wake Up Call #161)

Good Morning
it's time to get dirty
God doesn't respect a clean jersey

∞

(Wake Up Call #162)

Good Morning
it's time to pick a side
do you want to win or lose?
I don't care about what else is going on
today you must choose
are you in this to the end
or are you in this to pretend?
are you trying to be the boss
or are you just looking for more friends?
are you trying to be profitable
or just popular?
are you trying to make it happen
or are you just a gossiper?
it's time to pick a side
do you want to win or lose?
I don't care about what else is going on
TODAY YOU MUST CHOOSE!

∞

(Wake Up Call #163)

Good Morning
if you want that warrior status
you must go into battle
you must put your life on the line
to take the warrior's mantle
you must channel your God force
if you want the title of champion
because only a select group
can sit amongst God's pantheon

∞

(Wake Up Call #164)

Good Morning
take control of your life
never give anyone else the reins
this world is your domain
lay claim to all that it contains

∞

(Wake Up Call #165)

Good Morning
you're a tsunami set loose
a second gun hidden in the boot
a raw revolutionary
knee deep in the grassroots
you can't be stopped
you can't be derailed
no matter how they come at you
you will prevail

∞

(Wake Up Call #166)

Good Morning
you're going to need a strong
and fully functional
fuck it switch!

∞

(Wake Up Call #167)

Good Morning
inhale the feeling of appreciation
glorious jubilation
exhale the wonderment
of abundant inspiration
your new life is the culmination
of patience and dedication
this is the confirmation
that you're a living affirmation

(Wake Up Call #168)

Good Morning
be a festive celebration
be a beacon
be the transformation
be freedom
be the formless form
be the reincarnation
be the endless conversation
be creation

∞

(Wake Up Call #169)

Good Morning
enjoy this beautiful day
make the most of this beautiful day
smile bright on this beautiful day
laugh hard on this beautiful day
make love on this beautiful day
make life on this beautiful day
make a friend on this beautiful day
make amends on this beautiful day
fly high on this beautiful day
make some money on this beautiful day
help somebody on this beautiful day
thank God for life on this beautiful day

∞

(Wake Up Call #170)

Good Morning
even your greatest goals
are not worth your humanity

∞

(Wake Up Call #171)

Good Morning
if they can walk away from you
you can walk away from them
never beg anyone to love you
or be your friend
if they can't see your heart
let them wander aimless in the dark
don't let these snakes and sharks
stop you from making your mark

∞

(Wake Up Call #172)

Good Morning
sober the hell up
shake off that shit
without a clear mind
you can't keep your torches lit
you can't hit the ball
you can't put any points on the board
you will only get yourself hurt or killed
wielding a dull sword

∞

(Wake Up Call #173)

Good Morning
(repeat to yourself and then out loud)

today I will
clean up my house
today I will
straighten all my bullshit out
today I will
reopen my mind and heart
today I will
make a brand-new start

∞

(Wake Up Call #174)

Good Morning
(repeat to yourself and then out loud)

today is the day
that I confront my inner demons
I can't take my negative obsessions
into my next season
if I need some treatment
I'll be strong enough to get some treatment
keeping my torment, a secret
blocks and stops my future achievements

∞

(Wake Up Call #175)

Good Morning
(repeat to yourself and then out loud)

today
I will not feed my anxieties
today
I will focus on my priorities
today
I will not indulge in petty concerns
today
I will focus on my positive returns
today
I will not give the haters my time
today
I will focus on polishing my shine
today
I will survive depressions testing
today
I will treat my life like a supreme blessing

∞

(Wake Up Call #176)

Good Morning
(repeat to yourself and then out loud)

today I will hold myself accountable
for my mistakes and transgressions
today I will not make any excuses
for not heeding God's lessons
today I will cut off
all weak signals transmitted
today I will reject the company
of the hateful and wicked

∞

(Wake Up Call #177)

Good Morning
(repeat to yourself and then out loud)

today I will apologize
for all the lies I've told
today I will repent
for the trust and time, I stole
today I will listen
more than I talk
today I will finally
walk the walk

∞

(Wake Up Call #178)

Good Morning
(repeat to yourself and then out loud)

today I will
stop fighting the will of God
today I will
will pick up his divine rod
today I will
loose the extra weight
today I will
cut off all the fakes
today I will
stand firm as the mighty oak tree
today I will
be the best version of me

∞

(Wake Up Call #179)

Good Morning
(repeat to yourself and then out loud)

today I will
get up the nerve
today I will
get everything that I deserve
today I will
make the right choice
today I will
listen to my inner voice
today I will
fly towards the horizon
today I will
be the Lion from Holy Mount Zion

∞

(Wake Up Call #180)

Good Morning
(repeat to yourself and then out loud)

today I will be
invincible
today I will be
unsinkable
today I will be
untouchable
today I will be
unmovable
today I will be
insurmountable
today I will be
indomitable
today I will be
unassailable
today I will be
unbreakable

∞

(Wake Up Call #181)

Good Morning
(repeat to yourself and then out loud)

today I will
defeat all my opposition
today I will
change my financial position
today I will
shine brighter and brighter
today I will
be the smarter fighter
today I will
live in the moment
today I will
defeat all my opponents

∞

(Wake Up Call #182)

Good Morning
(repeat to yourself and then out loud)

today I will
look in the mirror and love what I see
today I will
set myself free
today I will
declare my freedom
today I will
conquer all my inner demons
today I will
fight the righteous fight
today I will
live inside God's loving light

∞

(Wake Up Call #183)

Good Morning
your phone is supposed to be your servant
don't let it become your master

∞

(Wake Up Call #184)

Good Morning
don't believe everything you read
flowing inside your Twitter feed
they've sacrificed journalism
for speed
most of the news on Instagram
isn't worth a damn
doin' the knowledge
is still the best way
to avoid being programed

∞

(Wake Up Call #185)

Good Morning
don't get caught up
in the cult of personality
don't let them
infect your mentality
don't follow them on social media
don't get caught up in their lives
because just like the devil
everything they promote
are illusions and lies

∞

(Wake Up Call #186)

Good Morning
stop trying to get the attention
of people who ignore you!

∞

(Wake Up Call #187)

Good Morning
don't waste time thinking
about what was supposed to happen
and start dealing with and confronting
what IS happening RIGHT NOW!

∞

(Wake Up Call #188)

Good Morning
stop arguing with people
who LOVE to argue

∞

(Wake Up Call #189)

Good Morning
accept the fact that not everybody
is going to understand you
get you, or accept you
just keep moving forward
regardless of the response or lack thereof

∞

(Wake Up Call #190)

Good Morning
LOVE YOURSELF OUT LOUD!

∞

(Wake Up Call #191)

Good Morning
stop starting fights in empty rooms!

∞

(Wake Up Call #192)

Good Morning
when you don't know
or can't remember who you are
it's easy to convince you
to accept less than you deserve

(Wake Up Call #193)

Good Morning
SAGE that bullshit
right out of your LIFE!

∞

(Wake Up Call #194)

Good Morning
stop putting your dreams, plans,
and goals on the backburner

∞

(Wake Up Call #195)

Good Morning
don't dumb yourself down
to let other people feel smart

∞

(Wake Up Call #196)

Good Morning
don't let the wrong person
or group wake you up

∞

(Wake Up Call #197)

Good Morning
God created you to CREATE
and be GREAT!

∞

(Wake Up Call #198)

Good Morning
be happy and excited to be alive
spend your time wisely
choose your words carefully
soak up the variety
never talk arrogantly
think intelligently
walk precisely
and always be Godly

∞

(Wake Up Call #199)

Good Morning
share your rhythm
share your vibrations
share your instruments
share your communications
share your arrangements
share your melodies
share your frequencies
share your symphonies

∞

(Wake Up Call #200)

Good Morning
(repeat to yourself and then out loud)

I believe that all life is equal
I believe that we're all one people
I believe that all life is valuable
I believe that anything is possible

∞

(Wake Up Call #201)

Good Morning
don't let your anger
consume you
don't let your pain
ruin you
don't let childhood memories
haunt you
don't let yesterday
destroy you
don't let your enemies
in your home
don't let the media
turn you into a drone
don't let the harassment
stop you
don't let America's racism
define you

∞

(Wake Up Call #202)

Good Morning
never relinquish
your childlike wonder and magic

∞

(Wake Up Call #203)

Good Morning
protect all children
from harm
protect all children
from the media's duplicitous charms
protect all children
from doubters and cynics
protect all children
from the devils lies and tricks

∞

(Wake Up Call #204)

Good Morning
help all children
find the best within them
help all children
see that true love never ends
help all children
heal life's deep scars
help all children
reach for the stars

(Wake Up Call #205)

Good Morning
being a boss is more than a hashtag
or a meme on IG
being a boss is having the power
to define your own destiny
being a boss isn't making fake calls
on a disconnected money phone
being a boss is owning and controlling
your own land and home
being a boss is helping others
uplifting your sisters and brothers
creating new opportunities
for the next generation to discover
a real boss creates new traditions
gets new acquisitions
establishes new universal definitions
for more harmonious conditions

∞

(Wake Up Call #206)

Good Morning
you've come too far
to even think about going back
the finish line is right in front of you
it's just a few more laps
everything is about to pay off
everything is about to come to fruition
the person in the mirror
is your only true competition
you can make it
you will make it
everything is right in front of you
reach out and take it
you've come too far
to even think about going back
the finish line is right in front of you
it's just a few more laps

∞

(Wake Up Call #207)

Good Morning
don't indulge the hateful
even if you're benefiting from them
don't support the dividers
even if your success stems from them
don't give cover to the warmongers
even if you agree with some of them
don't protect the blood suckers of the poor
even if you're in love with them

∞

(Wake Up Call #208)

Good Morning
don't set your life's course
by the dimly lit stars
of another person's opinion of you

∞

(Wake Up Call #209)

Good Morning
remember this universal fact of life:
it will **NEVER** be easy!

but that's okay beloved,
because if it were easy
it wouldn't be worth your trouble
or your time

∞

(Wake Up Call #210)

Good Morning
don't get hung up on yesterday
even if it was the best day of your life

∞

(Wake Up Call #211)

Good Morning
don't let the things you own, own you

∞

(Wake Up Call #212)

Good Morning
keep yourself plugged into God
s/he is your truest and purest
source of power

∞

(Wake Up Call #213)

Good Morning
have as much fun as humanly possible
but take life deadly serious

∞

(Wake Up Call #214)

Good Morning
open the floodgates
put on your breastplate
it isn't how well you can debate
it's how much you can demonstrate
how much can you add to life
how much can you offer humanity
if you want to change the world for the better
activate your audacious audacity

∞

(Wake Up Call #215)

Good Morning
keep a healthy dose
of paranoia and skepticism
in this era of
democratic Fascism
political mass hypnotism
social media narcissism
never choose academic smartness
over experience and wisdom
keep your antenna's up
keep your bullshit detector on
make sure you're on the right side
when the weapons are drawn

∞

(Wake Up Call #216)

Good Morning
you have the God given right
to be here

∞

(Wake Up Call #217)

Good Morning
NEVER abdicate your God given right
to defend yourself and your family

∞

(Wake Up Call #218)

Good Morning
be extremely selective on who you allow
in your heart
in your mind
in your body
and in your spirit
if they're not leading with love
speaking with love
acting with love
living with love
PUT THEM THE FUCK OUT!

∞

(Wake Up Call #219)

Good Morning
depression is real, dangerous, and deadly
don't take it lightly
the physical and spiritual cost
is too pricy
if you feel that gravity coming on you
reach out for help
scream out for help
if nobody comes
get up and get yourself some help
don't be embarrassed
don't be ashamed
lift your head up
you are **NOT** the blame
you WILL survive this
you WILL survive this
listen to me Beloved
YOU WILL SURVIVE THIS!

∞

(Wake Up Call #220)

Good Morning
YOU MATTER
YOU'RE NEEDED
YOU'RE WANTED
YOU'RE LOVED

(repeat 10 times to yourself)

I MATTER
I'M NEEDED
I'M WANTED
I'M LOVED

∞

(Wake Up Call #221)

Good Morning
love is stronger than hate
don't fall for the devil's bait
love is stronger than hate
have the fortitude to look evil in the face
I know it's daunting
I know it feels too much to take
but this is a truth that they can't negate
LOVE IS STRONGER THAN HATE!

∞

(Wake Up Call #222)

Good Morning
spend the overwhelming majority
of your time offline

∞

(Wake Up Call #223)

Good Morning
just showing up is a form of winning

∞

(Wake Up Call #224)

Good Morning
start making new mistakes

∞

(Wake Up Call #225)

Good Morning
protect your cipher
from the destructive people
that you hate
and from the destructive people
that you love

∞

(Wake Up Call #226)

Good Morning
your self-love and self-care come's first

∞

(Wake Up Call #227)

Good Morning
you don't have to answer every call
you can be discriminating with your time
you don't have to respond to all pleas
you can block people from your mind
put a high premium on your privacy
you can enter and leave society
giving everyone unlimited access
will bring you a world of stress and anxiety

∞

(Wake Up Call #228)

Good Morning
have more than one plan
choose more than one weapon
don't be slow to grow
expand your perceptions
backup your hard drives
use the truth and lies
cuz the way to survive
will never be cut and dry

∞

(Wake Up Call #229)

Good Morning
don't panic
think panoramic
once you understand the mechanics
you can conquer the planet
study mathematics
research the semantics
when your theories are practiced
you can conquer the planet

∞

(Wake Up Call #230)

Good Morning
don't be a nigga
no matter how cool and profitable
they make it appear to be

∞

(Wake Up Call #231)

Good Morning
before you can do the thing
you must become the thing
it was said before me
that thoughts are things
so, if you're not trying to be it
step away from it
because you're going to confuse
low plateaus with lofty summits

∞

(Wake Up Call #232)

Good Morning
always remember that good manners
can prevent misunderstandings and murder

∞

(Wake Up Call #233)

Good Morning
work for the glory of God
and not for the jealously and envy of man

∞

(Wake Up Call #234)

Good Morning
cancel cancel culture
bring that bullshit to a closure
some of us get wiser
when God allows us to get older
life's a roller coaster
we go higher and lower
most of our older twitter feeds
contain ignorant foul odors
but some of us get sober
and act with greater respect and esteem
if you support cancel culture
how do lost souls grow and get redeemed?

∞

(Wake Up Call #235)

Good Morning
timing is important
but don't waste time
waiting for the perfect time
because time will pass you by

∞

(Wake Up Call #236)

Good Morning
don't bow down to graven images
or mimic the devil's lineage
cuz if you want your life to be limitless
just honor God's privileges
take these words serious
don't be oblivious
cuz when you understand
the beautiful and the hideous
life will cease to be so mysterious

∞

(Wake Up Call #237)

Good Morning
don't be afraid to be disliked

∞

(Wake Up Call #238)

Good Morning
keep your heart open
don't be led astray by the broken
every moment won't be golden
but you're still one of the chosen

∞

(Wake Up Call #239)

Good Morning
without God, love, passion, desire, peace,
happiness, joy, laughter, sympathy, empathy,
intimacy, faith, family, friends, forgiveness,
truth, music, old age, variety, freedom,
justice, and equality, none of this is worth it

∞

(Wake Up Call #240)

Good Morning
be earnest
don't be nervous
summon your powers
everything is at your service
we all get scared
we all feel unprepared
but if you weren't ready
God wouldn't have placed you there
you're valuable
you're worthy
you got this
no need to worry
and we all get scared
we all feel unprepared
but if you weren't ready
God wouldn't have placed you there

∞

ABOUT THE AUTHOR

Carl Born Free Wharton was born and primarily raised in Philadelphia, Pennsylvania. He grew up in West Philly in a so-called "middle class" area called Wynnefield. He spent his formative years toggling in between the "Field" and down "The Bottom" at his Beloved Grandmother's (Pauline Ramsey) house on 38th & Poplar. The harsh dichotomies and undeniable similarities between these two neighborhoods taught and showed him graphically the range of black life during the 70's, 80's and 90's. He knew a life before the crack era and one after it struck. Witnessing the horror of this man-made plague created inside his soul a relentless conscious perspective that was born to stand on the frontlines of the struggle for freedom, justice, and equality.

The fabric of his community was forever changed during the governmental assault of guns, drugs, and miseducation, and Born was determined to find out who was responsible for these horrendous crimes. Since he was raised and came of age during Hip Hop's Cultural revolution, he understands the supreme importance of the written and spoken word. His love of reading and exploring the great pantheon of black writers and other great literary figures set him on the path of becoming a lifelong scribe. Born wants to communicate and connect with the reader's heart by invoking raw emotions and

holding up a mirror, so we can examine ourselves and the world around us.
Love is the connective tissue that unites everything that he does and writes about. Love is the fire that burns brilliantly in his heart. Born loves to write and build on a variety of classical and contemporary ideas and thoughts but his greatest desire is to compel the reader to get the hell up and confront this life right here and right now! He started his own publishing company, **Conscious Commentary Publishing LLC**. in 2018 to ensure that he never has to water down his perspective or compromise his vision. At the end of the day, Born Free wants US to get up and activate our activism, and use our God given talents to bring love and light to a world increasingly becoming dark.

Coming sooner than you think!

**The Book of Born Free
The Wisdom of Living
Right Now! Vol. 2**

**Follow Born Free
on all social media platforms
#therealbornfree**

**Contact
therealbornfree@gmail.com**

BONUS
WAKE UP CALLS
ONE thru TEN

(BONUS WAKE UP CALLS ONE)

Good Morning
increase your capacity
for sympathy and empathy
let the love for others
open your heart to spiritual ecstasy
love yourself
your love is wealth
take your love
off your fearful shelf
I'm not telling you to be naïve
or open yourself up to be deceived
I'm just saying that caring for others
will help you achieve

∞

(BONUS WAKE UP CALLS TWO)

Good Morning
stop feeling sorry for yourself
stop licking old wounds
no more pity parties
get the fuck out of your bedroom
no one is immune to disappointment's
no one is completely clairvoyant
stay afloat and buoyant
it's going to be a long
and treacherous voyage

∞

(BONUS WAKE UP CALLS THREE)

Good Morning
be a **SOLUTIONARY**!

∞

(BONUS WAKE UP CALLS FOUR)

Good Morning
if you want to be successful
you can't be afraid of blood

∞

(BONUS WAKE UP CALLS FIVE)

Good Morning
if you want to be successful
you must give up
all your favorite bad habits

∞

(BONUS WAKE UP CALLS SIX)

Good Morning
if you want to be successful
you must stop blaming everybody else
for the events in your life

∞

(BONUS WAKE UP CALLS SEVEN)

Good Morning
even when you're asleep
#STAYWOKE
ignorance and white supremacy
is no fuckin' joke
they come in a billion different forms
they wear a billion different uniforms
keep your third eye open
when the broken spread omen emotions
you need sleep
but you need to stay prepared
so even when your eyes are closed
stay completely aware

∞

(BONUS WAKE UP CALLS EIGHT)

Good Morning
THINK!
but
DON'T OVER THINK!

∞

(BONUS WAKE UP CALLS NINE)

Good Morning
upgrade your conscious awareness
subdue your ego and arrogance
through conscious preparedness
you'll survive your exodus
as you pull back
your celestial bedspread
you'll find your daily bread
to clear the cobwebs from your head
because when you shed
all the depression and dread
there's no such thing
as the wrong side of the bed

∞

(BONUS WAKE UP CALLS TEN)

Good Morning
God has favored you
on this new and wondrous morn
you survived
yesterday's battles and storms
those deep scars will heal
those hurtful memories will fade
your success and prosperity
will no longer be delayed

∞

**Follow Born Free
on all social media platforms
#therealbornfree**

**Contact
therealbornfree@gmail.com**

**Support QVision
follow on IG and Fiverr @**

https://www.instagram.com/qvision223/

https://www.fiverr.com/qvision223

What the hell are you waiting for???

FIGHT BACK!!!!!!!!!!

LOVE BACK!!!!!!!!!!!!

FIGHT BACK!!!!!!!!!!

LOVE BACK!!!!!!!!!!!!

FIGHT BACK!!!!!!!!!!

LOVE BACK!!!!!!!!!!!!

FIGHT BACK!!!!!!!!!!

LOVE BACK!!!!!!!!!!!!

FIGHT BACK!!!!!!!!!!

LOVE BACK!!!!!!!!!!!!

FIGHT BACK!!!!!!!!!!

LOVE BACK!!!!!!!!!!!!

FIGHT BACK!!!!!!!!!!

LOVE BACK!!!!!!!!!!!!

www.ingramcontent.com/pod-product-compliance
Lightning Source LLC
Chambersburg PA
CBHW071303110426
42743CB00042B/1154